The American Pet Stock Standard of Perfection
Rabbits, Cavies and Fancy Mice and Rats

by American Fur Fancier's Association

with an introduction by Jackson Chambers

Self Reliance Books

Get more historic titles on animal and stock breeding, gardening and old fashioned skills by visiting us at:

http://selreliancebooks.blogspot.com/

Introduction

I am pleased to present yet another title in the "Cavies" series.

The work is in the Public Domain and is re-printed here in accordance with Federal Laws.

Though this work is a century old it contains much information on bees that is still pertinent today.

As with all reprinted books of this age that are intended to perfectly reproduce the original edition, considerable pains and effort had to be undertaken to correct fading and sometimes outright damage to existing proofs of this title. At times, this task is quite monumental, requiring an almost total "rebuilding" of some pages from digital proofs of multiple copies. Despite this, imperfections still sometimes exist in the final proof and may detract from the visual appearance of the text.

I hope you enjoy reading this book as much as I enjoyed making it available to readers again.

Jackson Chambers

FOREWORD

The imperative need by everyone who may be interested in fancy pets for an authoritative publication presenting a definite standard of perfection for their guidance in intelligently striving for the "ideal" animal, has prompted The American Fur Fanciers' Association to offer to pet stock fanciers this Guide.

The information contained herein has been compiled from noted works on pet stock, specialty clubs, and other associations of prominent men and women who have devoted a goodly portion of their life work to perfecting animals up to that standard which man believes Nature should have adopted in its natural law of selection.

Without some description, the novice would have difficulty in comprehending the relative points designated for the several component parts which go to make up the IDEAL of each variety. Under each variety, therefore, may be found such information as should tend to give the novice a clearer conception of those points which need careful observance in the breeding of fancy pets for exhibition purposes.

The collection of photographs from which the illustrations were reproduced are believed to be some of the finest obtainable, and while many of them appear to be nearly perfect, as to markings, etc., it should be understood that they are offered, not as the IDEAL, but as a guide to the novice, so that he may the better picture in his mind the standard of points provided for each variety.

It is to be regretted that in former years fanciers did not maintain more perfect records of their experiments that the fancy might know just how and by what crosses the various breeds have been evolved. It is therefore necessary for the novice to associate himself with the more learned fanciers by joining the Pet Stock Association, which furnishes gratis a subscription to its official magazine, so that he may be saved the years of time already spent in perfecting our fancy pets.

The Association expresses its appreciation to all who have so generously rendered assistance in this work, especially to those who, by their perseverance, have assisted in evolving the many new varieties of pet stock which grace our show benches. It is to these FANCIERS that THE AMERICAN FUR FANCIERS' ASSOCIATION dedicates

THE AMERICAN PET STOCK STANDARD OF PERFECTION AND OFFICIAL GUIDE.

OFFICERS AND MEMBERS OF GOVERNING BOARD FOR 1915

President—J. Henri Wagner, 1909 North Capitol Street, Washington, D. C.

First Vice-President—Albert G. Sherwood, 59 Main Street, Nyack, New York.

Second Vice-President—T. A. Martin, Jr., Freeport, Long Island, New York.

Secretary-Treasurer—John Ruckstuhl, Jr., 115 Hague Street, Jersey City Heights, New Jersey.

Specialty Representatives

Fancy Rabbits—F. V. Kellogg, Closter, New Jersey.

Belgian Hares—H. K. Filor, West Haverstraw, New York.

Fancy Mice—S. Chichester Lloyd, 51½ Sumpter Street, Brooklyn, New York.

Smooth Cavies—Henry A. Regel, 311 North Forty-second Street, Camden, New Jersey.

Peruvian Cavies—Miss B. Hendrickson, Rockville Center, Long Island.

Abyssinian Cavies—Dudley Coakley, 369 Main Street, Waltham, Massachusetts.

THE FANCY RABBIT

We learn from Mr. George A. Townsend, the English Judge and Author, that the first exhibition of fancy rabbits on record was held at Gravesend, in 1859, when classes were provided for Lops only. Slowly, but steadily, the fancy rabbit grew in popularity among the sportsmen until 1888, when the United Kingdom Rabbit Club was formed. From this time the fancy grew by leaps and bounds, many specialty clubs springing up all over the world to foster the several varieties. These clubs were organized principally

ENGLISH LOP RABBIT (Baker Brothers)

to promote the fancy, provide exhibitions in various sections of the country, and draw up standards for the guidance of the fancier. Crude as were the several breeds when first appearing on the show bench, they have been developed through the medium of patient and persevering effort until now we have a collection of the rarest specimens of animal of life which imagination can depict.

ENGLISH LOP

The origin of the Lop Rabbit (commonly known as the "Lop Ear Rabbit") is not known, although it can be traced back a hundred years. In 1859 fancy rabbit societies existed throughout England, the only breed at that time appearing on the show bench being the Lop. Twenty inches was considered extremely long for the ears of the Lop of the seventies; while to this day twenty-eight inch ears are not uncommon. Width of ear has also been one of great advancement, the best of today measuring seven and one-half inches.

In the early age of the Lop fancy much attention was paid to the color of the rabbit, but during recent years so much stress has been laid to the length and width of ear that the matter of color development has been sadly neglected.

There are the "Selfs," comprising Black, Blue Grey, Sooty, Sooty Fawn, and Golden Fawn; and the "Broken" colors, which consist of Black and White, Blue and White, Grey and White, Fawn and White, and Tortoise and White. The "Self" colors should be absolutely free from white or any other than the "self color" hairs which make up the color. White toes, white star on forehead, or white (putty) nose are defects which warrant severe cuts as demerits in competition.

In the "Broken" colors the head should be self-colored, with the exception of a white star on the forehead. The saddle covers practically the whole of the body except the shoulders, which should have two or three patches or spots of white. The underneath parts of the Lop, from jaws to thighs, should be white, as well as all four feet, but the white visible on the top portion of the Lop should not be too prominent.

The study of color breeding in the Lop is one of the deepest interest and much discretion is necessary to produce correct color coincident with ear measurement and size of dew-lap, which latter characteristic is also a very important feature of the Lop.

STANDARD OF POINTS

	*S.L.C.	*A.L.C.
EAR Length	15	25
EAR Width	15	20
SUBSTANCE AND SHAPE, i.e., strong, stout and clear of blemishes, the tip wide and round, not pointed	5	5
SHAPE AND CARRIAGE of rabbit........	10	5
COLOR AND MARKINGS of rabbit.......	15	10
CONDITION	10	10
STRAIGHT FEET AND TAIL	10	10
EYE, CLEAR AND BOLD	10	10
SIZE AND WEIGHT, large as possible.....	10	5

* S. L. C.=Specific Length Classes.
* A. L. C.=Any Length Classes.

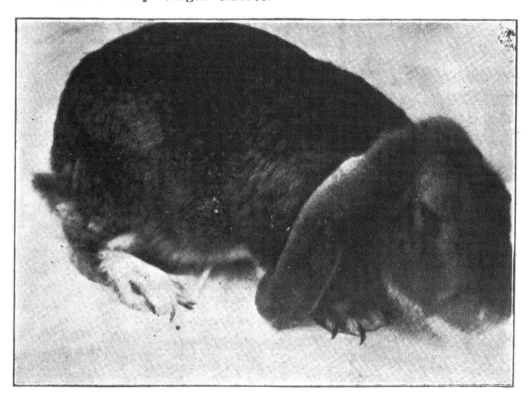

FRENCH LOP RABBIT (Henry A. Regel)

FRENCH LOP

STANDARD OF POINTS

EARS—Length 16 to 18 inches.........................	20
HEAD—Short and thick	10
EYES—Large and bold	5
BODY—Large and slightly arched, does to have dewlap....	15

LEGS AND FEET—Straight and heavy-boned 10
SIZE AND WEIGHT—To be as great as possible; does 13
    pounds; bucks 12 pounds............................. 30
CONDITION—Flesh firm, coat smooth.................. 10
    DISQUALIFICATION: Permanent wry tail or feet.

BELGIAN HARE RABBIT (Geo. A. Townsend--Practical Rabbit Keeping)

BELGIAN HARE

This variety is referred to as the "Belgian Hare," but, except as regards similarity of type, it has no pretensions to be a hare. The Belgian in the early years of the fancy was a very large rabbit, in color resembling the wild English Hare, having black hairs to produce a "ticked" effect and ear lacing. The Belgian of today resembles the wild hare in body, limbs, head and ears; bold, clear, eye; but a color of rich golden tan, broken only by wavy ticking peculiar to no other variety.

It has been asserted that the variety originated in Belgium or in Germany, and that in the early stages of development it was crossed with other giant varieties to produce size and weight. Forty years ago the "dew-lap" was required in the Belgian, but as type progressed the dew-lap was discarded as faulty and is now prohibited. The demand today is for golden tan color all over the rabbit's body, belly, head, ears, flanks and feet. The head should be long and narrow, legs straight and fine in bone. Length of body is desirable, as it shows up beautifully on a well-matured Belgian of the standard weight, eight pounds. The "ticking" or black-tipped hairs scattered profusely over the rabbit, presenting a wavy appearance, is a strict require-

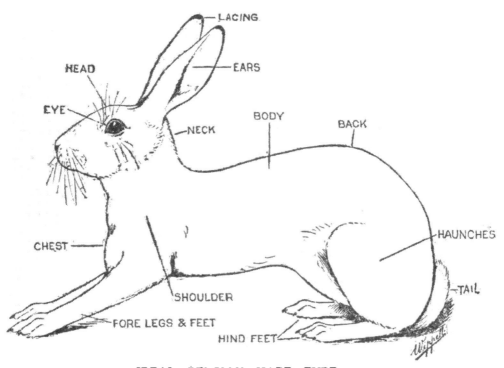

IDEAL BELGIAN HARE TYPE.
SHOWING THE REQUIRED SHAPE AND STYLE.

(Fur und Feather)

ment. Other than this there are no markings to breed for, practically everything depending on shape and color for the making of the true type of a winning Belgian. Its condition, as the standard prescribes, should manifest plenty of flesh and muscle, healthy skin, and the coat lying close to the body, of silky texture and shining bright as a mirror. The abdomen should hang very little lower than the chest, and when the rabbit is at "attention" plenty of space should be seen between the fore and hind legs. This "style" can be produced principally by handling, grooming, the use of hurdles in hutches or runs, to prevent the rabbit from becoming "baggy" or "squatty" in shape. It likewise hardens the muscle and increases the length of limb and body.

"Flakey" feet or white hairs in the coat of the Belgian constitute imperfections that should be strongly cut in judging.

STANDARD OF POINTS

COLOR—Rich Rufus Red (not dark smudgy color), carried well down sides and hindquarters, and as little white under jaws as possible 20
SHAPE—Body long, thin, well-tucked-up flank, and well-ribbed up, back slightly arched, loins well rounded, not choppy, head rather lengthy, muscular chest, tail straight, not screwed (either temporarily or permanently), and altogether a racy appearance 20
TICKING—Wavy in appearance and plentiful.............. 10
EARS—About five inches long, thin, well laced on tips, and as far down outside edges as possible, good color inside and outside and well set on............................ 10
EYES—Hazel color, large, round, bright and bold.......... 10
LEGS AND FEET—Fore feet and legs long, straight, slender, well-colored and free from white bars; hind feet well colored 10
WITHOUT DEWLAP 10
SIZE AND WEIGHT—About eight pounds............... 5
CONDITION—Healthy, not fat, but flesh firm like a race-horse, and a good quality of fur...................... 5

SILVER

Silver Grey, Silver Fawn, Silver Brown

There are three classes of Silver Rabbits, as above indicated.

Divers theories have been advanced regarding the origin of the Silver Grey. One is that it was developed from the English wild grey rabbit, known as the "Silver Sprig," another that it was imported from Siam because of its fur-bearing quality. It was first placed on exhibition about 1860, but it was not until 1899 that the Silver Club of England was formed for the purpose of pushing the Silver Fancy.

The Silver Grey, like the other Silvers, should be lively and bright in disposition; the silvering should be neither light, nor dark, but medium. Short coated rabbits are usually the most ideal in bright and sharp silvering—white hairs intermixed with the colored hairs—the ground color being a rich blue-black. Rustiness should be avoided. This is most frequently noticed on the haunches and inside the fore feet. Particular attention should be paid to the evenness of silvering on the feet, cheeks, jaws and whisker-beds. The ears should be neat in shape and not too long. The silvering should extend evenly over the whole furred portion of the ears, right up to the edges, and of exactly the

SILVER FAWN RABBIT (Bell and Heaton)

same shade of the body. The claws should match the body color, and while white claws are not a disqualification, they should be heavily penalized in competition. While the tail is usually darker than the body, it is desirable and advantageous to strive to match the body.

The Silver Fawn, once known as the Silver Cream, is thought to have originated in France. As the Fawn has been made by crossing several varieties, uniformity and evenness of color are difficult to attain. This is equally true with Browns. The color, or shade, is difficult to de-

9

scribe, but is sometimes named "silver-orange." "Putty-noses," disqualification; barred feet, smudgy face, and bad undercolor should be avoided in all of the Silvers and heavily penalized.

The Silver Brown is also a "made" rabbit and was produced after the Fawn. It is supposed to be a cross between

IDEAL SILVER GREY RABBIT (Fur and Feather)

a Silver Grey Buck and a Belgian Doe, and recrossed with a Grey Buck for the silvering. The brown should be void of the blue cast to the color which is often noticed. It is made up of four distinct colors—slate-blue, brown, black, and white—the white being the silvering and the black the ticking. The slate-blue should start at the root of the fur, extending halfway up each hair, the end being a bright, rich chestnut color. No pale blue or white color should be visible when the fur is turned back with the fingers. The hind feet should match the fore feet. Avoid a coarse, baggy rabbit, with long coat and ears.

STANDARD OF POINTS

UNDERCOLOR—GREY—Deep, rich blue-black:
    FAWN—Deep, bright orange, free from brick color:
    BROWN—Deep, rich chestnut 25
SILVERING—Even throughout 20
TICKING—Sharp, even and bright 15
COAT—Short and full 15
EARS—Neat and well set on, and
EYES—Bold and bright 10
CONDITION AND SHAPE—Flesh firm and free from bagginess: weight about six pounds...................... 15

ENGLISH RABBIT (Geo. A. Townsend- Practical Rabbit Keeping)

ENGLISH

The English is one of the most recently "made" varieties. It was undoubtedly started from the common English or "Butterfly Smut" rabbit. It made its appearance on the show bench about 1890 under the name of "English" rabbit.

In its early stages the English rabbit was a black rabbit, with splashes of white. The present-day English is white, with clear, definitely placed markings and spots. The markings were not standardized until 1891 when the National English Rabbit Club was formed. It is conceded by all fanciers that the English rabbit has made more rapid strides towards perfection than any other variety, in spite of the fact that more points are necessary to be sought for than any other variety of rabbit. In addition to shape and color, which are the principal requirements in most varieties, we have the beautiful markings distributed all over the animal in such a manner as to create quite a sensation to the eye and a most enjoyable treat for both novice and layman to behold.

The English of the past generation was known as "Butterfly Smut," which it is supposed derived its name from the butterfly-shaped nose, the tail portion extending up the fore face, exactly in the middle, while the wings extend to the sides of the nose, but not quite to the lower lip or jaw. The "butterfly" should be absolutely solid in color and should have no stray colored hairs.

The spots encircling the eyes should be about the size of a half-dollar, whereas the cheek-spots should be about half the size of a dime, and clear from the eye circles.

The ears should be neat and free from white hairs, and not over four inches in length.

The remaining part of the head, up to the base of the ears, should be perfectly white and free from any stray colored hairs.

The saddle should consist of an unbroken colored streak, beginning with a narrow stripe at the base of the ears, and should gradually widen towards the center of the back where the width should be the greatest, and finish with a very narrow stripe at the end of the tail. The edges of the saddle should be ragged, which is commonly known as "herring-boned."

The body and loin markings are divided into three parts and are defined as follows:

1. The body markings are those connecting the end of

the chain with the loin spots and should be equally distributed in small spots below the saddle.

2. Loin markings furnish the hind quarters of the rabbit and should not exceed the size of a ten-cent piece.

3. The chain commences with a single spot about the size of a pea below and back of the ear, gradually increasing in size and number until they join the loin spots, where they should be the largest, and then diminish in size again towards the end of the loins.

The other parts of the body, shoulders and chest should be entirely free from markings.

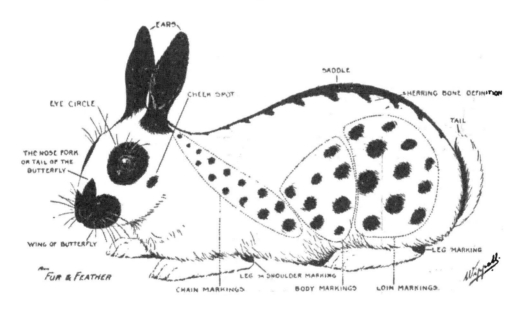

IDEAL ENGLISH RABBIT (Fur and Feather)

STANDARD OF POINTS

Head Markings

NOSE—Perfect butterfly smut............................. 15
EYE—Circle around each eye.............................. 8
    Spots to be clear from eye circle.................... 5
EARS—Neat and free from white hairs, and not more than
    four inches in length................................ 5

Body Markings

NEAT SADDLE, to be herring-boned and clear in any solid
    color 10
SIDES OF BODY to be evenly patched with spots which
    should not touch saddle 12
CHAIN MARKINGS, as even as possible on each side..... 12

13

LEG MARKINGS, one distinct spot on each leg; front
    5 points, hind 2 points.................................... 7
BELLY or teat SPOTS, six in number.................... 6
COLOR 10
SIZE AND SHAPE, six to eight pounds and between Silver
    and Belgian 5
CONDITION, good coat and firm in flesh................. 5
    DISQUALIFICATION: Putty noses.

DUTCH

The Dutch rabbit originated in Holland, where it was bred principally for table purposes, little attention being given to color stops until the fancy took the breeding of the Dutch, and today it is claimed to be the most popular breed in that country. The Dutch is bred in five standard colors: Black, Blue, Tortoise, Steel or Dark Grey, and Light Grey. Occasionally may be seen Blue-Greys, Blue Fawns, and Yellow.

DUTCH RABBIT (Henry A. Regel)

Seventy points out of a hundred are allotted to color and color-stops. It is manifest therefore that the color is the principal feature to breed for.

The blaze is that part of the white marking on the head which comes down the center of the face, dividing the cheeks. It should come through the ears and gradually widen as it gets down the face, being wedge-shaped.

The cheek markings should come down close to the whisker beds, but not touch them, and run along the edge of the jaw and around the base of the ears. They should be round and void of any stray white hairs on the edge of the jaw.

The length of the ears should be in proportion to the body, neatness being the principal factor.

The collar is the white fur between the neck and the saddle.

The saddle is the point where the collar ceases and the colored fur begins on the upper part of the body, which should be just behind the shoulders and should go in a perfectly straight line around the body, more than one-half of the body being colored. The undercut is the under part of the body, and is a continuation of the saddle, which should run close behind the fore legs, but not touch them. The colored portion of the body should extend from the saddle marking over the hind quarters and tail, stopping about one and a half inches from the toes, the remainder of each foot being white. Both feet should be exactly alike; the division should run all around the foot.

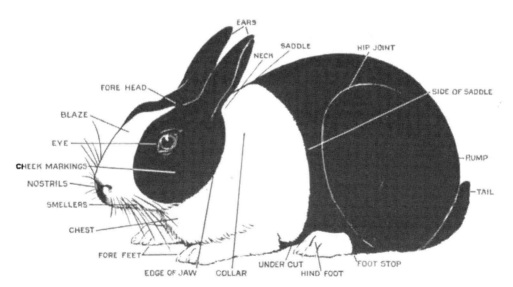

IDEAL DUTCH MARKED RABBIT (Fur and Feather)

The color of the iris in the eye of the Dutch should be as nearly of the shade of the color of the rabbit as possible, and should be free of specks or discoloration. Disqualification: Small specks on eyes, discolored or wall eyes. Distinct spots in the white portions, or flesh markings, and if the rabbit weighs over five and a half pounds, should be heavily penalized.

15

As to size and shape, the Dutch may be described as small and cobby; the body short, neat and compact, with the head in proportion. The coat should be sleek and bright.

STANDARD OF POINTS

BLAZE AND CHEEKS 15
NECK, clean 10
SADDLE 10
UNDERCUT 10
FEET STOPS 15
EARS, proportionate to size of body................... 10
EYES, clear and free from defects and color of body marking 5
COLOR, sound and level 10
SIZE, not to exceed 5½ pounds; SHAPE, cobby; CONDITION, firm 15

HAVANA RABBITS (Geo. A. Townsend—Practical Rabbit Keeping)

HAVANA

The Havana, like many of the other varieties, derived its color through accidental breeding. While some have believed that it originated in France, one authority states that it was bred in 1898 from black and white marked common

16

table rabbits in Holland. They did not, however, become very popular until 1910, when the English fanciers took hold of the Havana and when the Crystal Palace Show had a large class of Havanas.

The Havana is brown all over, including the belly, the pale grey undercolor being only at the base of the fur next to the skin and therefore not visible unless the fur is parted with the fingers. It is lively, active and very shy. The color is very susceptible to fading when kept in the sunlight, or in continuous damp weather, when the brown fades into a reddish color and becomes patchy. White hairs on the back or on ears; and failing in color on chest, sides of body and hind legs should be heavily penalized.

STANDARD OF POINTS

COLOR—A rich, bright brown all over, with undercoat of
    pale grey 30
SHAPE AND SIZE—Exceedingly fine and elegant, some-
    what like the Black and Tan, head and neck medium;
    weight, when full grown, not to exceed 5½ pounds..... 30
EARS—Four inches long, fine in substance, small, straight
    and carried upright 10
FEET—Very slender and straight, with brown toenails.... 10
EYES—Large, the color of the fur, showing a red light in
    pupil, yet having a soft and gentle expression......... 5
COAT—Short, fine and silky 10
CONDITION—Healthy, clean, firm in flesh.............. 5

POLISH

Several sources of origin have been accredited to the Polish rabbit, but they are all merely matters of conjecture. It is believed, however, that its existence is due to a few of England's most prominent fanciers who entered the Polish in the shows about 1884. The most perfect specimens are said to have emanated from the Dutch rabbit. It is "an all quality" rabbit, void of the slightest suspicion of coarseness. It should weigh between 2½ and 3½ pounds, fine and neat body, and alert. The coat must be short and very fine in texture and lie very close and tight. The Polish should be short and plump; ears fine, thin, neat, nicely rounded, and covered with fine, short fur; head narrow and racy looking, with ears carried erect. The eyes should be bright, bold and blood color, while the feet and limbs should be neat, compact and free from coarseness. It should be pure white and of glossy appearance.

POLISH RABBITS (Geo. A. Townsend—Practical Rabbit Keeping)

STANDARD OF POINTS

SHAPE AND SIZE—Neat, compact and sprightly; weight
    2½ to 3½ pounds.................................... 25
COAT—Fine, close and short 25
COLOR—Pure white 15
EARS—Short, fine, well rounded, and covered, to touch all
    the way up without showing flange.................... 15
EYES—Bright, bold, and as near blood red as possible...... 15
CONDITION 5

IDEAL HEAD OF POLISH RABBIT, SHOWING CORRECT EARS
(Geo. A. Townsend—Practical Rabbit Keeping)

HIMALAYAN

The Himalayan has been found in the countries lying north and south of the Himalayan Mountains, and for that reason many people are of the belief that it originated there.

HIMALAYAN RABBIT (Geo. A. Townsend—Practical Rabbit Keeping)

This theory is disputed, however, by the fact that it also exists in China and was later introduced into Continental Europe as the "Russian Rabbit," "Egyptian Smut," "Chinese," "Antwerp," etc., and it was not until the Englishman took hold of the breeding of this variety that it received the name "Himalayan."

The color of the Himalayan's markings should be rich, velvety black, free of all brown tinge. The markings should be on the nose, ears, feet and tail. The nose marking should be large, well rounded, and come well up the face between the eyes, clean cut and distinct. The ears should be entirely black and well covered with fur; short, neat and tapering to the tips; set fairly close together and not carried apart. The feet should be black right to the top of the legs and cut clean there. The tail should also be black. The eye should be pink, bright and bold. Eye-stain is a disqualification.

The Himalayan should be snaky in shape (short and cobby rabbits should be heavily penalized), neat and small. The weight about five pounds.

STANDARD OF POINTS

EARS—Short, tapering and well set...................... 15
NOSE—Even and well up between eyes.................. 15
FRONT FEET—Long, slender and markings well up...... 15
HIND FEET—To correspond, markings well up hocks.... 25
EYES—Bold, bright and pink 5
TAIL—Neat, black all over 5
SHAPE—Snaky 5
COAT—Short, fine and pure white....................... 5
WEIGHT—About five pounds 5
CONDITION 5

BLUE IMPERIAL

Miss Mabel Illingworth, of Brentwood, England, introduced this variety of rabbit to the fancy. This was in 1898. It was brought about in this fashion. She mated a blue Lop doe to a white Angora, which resulted in a litter of pink-eyed whites, blue-fawns and self blues of a dark shade. All had upright ears. She then mated one of these young blue does to a very heavily marked blue-fawn Dutch buck, from which she got blues, and blue-fawns; some with white feet, noses or faces. She kept two all-blue does which she mated to a newly purchased dark blue Dutch, and crossed and re-crossed until she "created" the beautiful Blue Imperial which now adorns the show bench. Her "standard of excellence" needs no elaboration.

BLUE IMPERIAL, and its Originator (C. A. House—Rabbits and all About Them)

STANDARD OF POINTS

COLOR—An even dark blue over all...................... 30
SHAPE AND SIZE—Somewhat like the Belgian Hare;
    body long and graceful, shoulders compact, back gradu-

ally rising to haunches, which should be well rounded, tail long, head long and narrow, with neck of medium length; weight, when full grown, over six pounds, but not to exceed seven pounds............................ 30

LEGS AND FEET—Clean and straight, fine in bone, with dark toenails 5

EARS—Between four and five inches long, well covered with fur, round at the tips, carried erect and fairly close together 10

EYES—Large, bright, deep blue in color, matching the fur.. 15

COAT—Thick, soft and glossy, lying close to skin......... 5

CONDITION—Healthy, clean, firm and hard in flesh...... 5

IDEAL FLEMISH GIANT RABBIT DOE (C. A. House—Rabbits and all About Them)

FLEMISH GIANT

This, the largest exhibition variety of rabbit, is a native of Flanders, the lowlands of Belgium.

The Patagonian, from which the Flemish Giant was evolved, was bred in grey, brown-grey and black. Now we have the black, steel-grey and white.

The name "Flemish Giant" was manifestly given this variety because of its size, which is the principal point sought for in its breeding. Does weighing 21 pounds and bucks weighing 15 pounds have appeared on the show bench, but they are a rarity.

The head should be stout, full and shapely—"the bull-dog type of head"—resting on the dew-lap of doe, which should be large as possible in the Flemish.

There has been increasing inclination among fanciers to breed pure black Flemish Giants. The most favorite color, however, is the steel-grey, the production of which has caused size and weight to be neglected. This may not be worthy of criticism, moreover, as the two should go hand in hand in the breeding of fine specimens of Flemish Giants. As a consequence, to produce size and weight, black and any-other-color classes have been demanded by the fancy.

FLEMISH GIANT HEADS—On the left length and fineness, which are not desirable: on the right stoutness and strength, the bulldog type of head that is so much desired.

(C. A. House—Rabbits and all About Them)

The color, whatever it may be, should be clear and bright all over the rabbit, including the feet, shoulders, sides, hind-quarters and thighs, EXCEPT the belly, which should be white, but the white should not be visible when the rabbit is in position for judging. The tail should match the body color on top, and the white belly color underneath.

Putty nose, white toes, lop ears are disqualifications.

STANDARD OF POINTS

Steel Grey

SIZE AND WEIGHT—Bucks shall not be less than eleven pounds and does not less than thirteen pounds; size shall be considered irrespective of weight.............. 30

COLOR—Dark steel grey, with even or wavy ticking over the whole body, head, ears, chest and feet alike, except belly and under tail, which shall be white. Any grey, steel, sandy or other shade on belly or under tail, except a streak of grey in each groin, shall be penalized according to quality of competing specimens.................. 20

BODY—Large, roomy, squarely and heavily built; broad fore and hind quarters. Does shall have a dewlap, evenly carried 15

LEGS AND FEET—Shall be strong in bone, large and straight 15

HEAD AND EARS—Head shall be large, full and shapely; eye bold and dark brown in color; ears erect and moderately thick 10

CONDITION—Full short coat, firm in flesh and free from cold 10

Any Other Self Color

Same points as Steel Grey, except as to color, which may be any solid color.

ANGORA

The Angora rabbit, with its long, fleecy tresses, is in a class to itself. It is just the contrary to nearly all other varieties of rabbits, which, as a rule, require as short and close a coat as possible. It is supposed to have been originally found in Persia and Asia Minor, where also other long-haired animals, such as goats, sheep and cats are said to have originated. From thence they drifted into Switzerland and Belgium, where the peasants reared them principally for their wool, and later for use by the furriers.

It is bred in a number of colors, the most prominent of which is white. The other colors, of which few are bred, are Blue, Black, Grey and Fawn.

The coat should be uniformly long and the quality should be like fine, soft wool, and "not in any way open or cottony," so that when the rabbit is properly brushed it will have the appearance of a huge snowball, as the head is practically hidden from view. The ears should be short, thick and erect, well covered with hair, with tufts on the extreme ends. The legs and feet should be well covered with long hair, commonly called "well furnished." The head should be large and well rounded and a generous quantity of long hair should appear between and behind the ears. An Angora with a narrow-skulled head should be heavily penalized.

It is a recognized fact that the constant annoyance in faithful brushing has a tendency to keep down the size of the Angora. This is also attributed to the great amount of

ANGORA RABBIT (A. C. Westley)

strength going to the length of coat. And while size is therefore difficult to attain, stress should be laid on requiring cobby-shaped rabbits.

The eyes should be deep pink, large, bright and bold. The tail should be long and covered with long wool.

Unless the Angora is in good condition, its general qualifiscations will be correspondingly diminished. The coat must be clear of all mats or cots.

STANDARD OF POINTS

WOOL.—Texture as silky as possible.................... 30
    Length and Quality: Evenly thick all over (not to be matted) 25
FRONT—Full and prominent 10
EARS—Short, well woolled and tufted 10
SIZE AND SHAPE 15
CONDITION—Clean, well fed, healthy and well groomed.. 10

TAN RABBIT (C. A. House)

BLACK AND TAN—BLUE AND TAN

The Tan rabbit is one of the several varieties which have been introduced in the past twenty-five years. It made its appearance on the show bench in 1889. In 1891 the first club was formed for its advancement; but it was not until 1902 that real progress was made in introducing this variety into popular favor.

The description of the IDEAL Tan, Black or Blue, as given by the Tan Rabbit Club, is as follows (except as to color, the Blue is the same as Black where mentioned):

COLOR—No other color but Black and Tan (or Blue and Tan). No white or foreign color amongst either black or tan. The color, both in the black and the tan, should reach well to the skin.

26

DISTRIBUTION OF BLACK (Body Color) and TAN (Markings)—The head and cheeks to be black, that color reaching right up to the nose point, but with a ring of tan round each eye (eye circles). The shoulders (except immediately behind the ears), saddle, back, rump, sides and upper part of tail, black. All should be free from brindling except sides, and sides of rump, which should be thickly laced with long tan hairs (side brindling). The nostrils, jowl, chest, belly, flanks and under part of tail should be one solid mass of deep golden tan, inclining to red or mahogany tint; brightness of tan to be of greater importance than actual tint. The tan should be quite free from any mixture of soot or body color. The shoulders or neck, immediately behind the ears, should be tanned; wide near the ears and tapering to a fine point towards back, thus forming a triangle. This should be large enough to be partly seen, even when the rabbit's head is up. From the base of the triangle, near the ears, the tan should descend, and, if possible, meet the tan on the chest, thus forming a kind of band or collar around the neck. At the root of the ears, viewed from the front, two tan spots, known as "Pea Spots," should be seen; the larger these the better.

EARS—Short, fine, but not papery; carried erect, and close together. Outside, jet black, well covered with fur. Inside, faced with tan all around (if the whole insides are tanned, so much the better). Ears free from white tips, white hairs or brindling.

HIND LEGS—Rather short, and of medium thickness. The outer part of the leg, reaching from foot to rump, black; inner part rich tan. The division between black and tan should form an unbroken line right up the leg, free from raggedness. The tan on inner side to be quite free from spots, pencilling or bars of black. Toes wholly tanned.

FRONT LEGS—The lower front part black; as free from brindle as possible. The hinder parts and toes wholly tanned.

SHAPE—The shorter and more cobby in build the better.

WEIGHT OF ADULT—Three to four and one-half pounds.

27

COAT—Fairly short, laying well to the body, with a silky feel to the hand.

STANDARD OF POINTS

BLACK (or BLUE—in BLUE AND TANS), dense and sound		10
TAN—Deep rich		15
TRIANGLE	5	
FEET—Hind	10	
FEET—Front	5	
CHEST, FLANKS AND BELLY	10	
NOSTRILS, EYES AND JOWL	5	
EARS—Outer and inner margins	5	40
EARS—Short and black (except where noted otherwise)		10
SHAPE—Dutch		10
EYE—Full (Black in Black-and-Tans; Blue in Blue-and-Tans)		5
CONDITION		10

NEW ZEALAND RED DOE (From Domestic Pets, Julius R. Briggs, owner)

THE NEW ZEALAND RED

The New Zealand Red is the only one of the rabbit family that has been evolved in America. From what crosses it was made is not known, but from the spirit in which it is received by fanciers all over the country it is destined to become one of the standard varieties and one of the most popular in America. While it is spoken of mostly as a "utility" rabbit, its color and shape are conspicuous by their beauty. Disqualifications: Lopped or fallen ear, crooked feet, other than hazel eyes, wry tail. Does to have dew-lap evenly carried.

28

STANDARD OF POINTS

(Official Standard of National New Zealand Red Club)

COLOR—Even reddish buff, carried well down sides with
    whitish under body 30
WEIGHT AND SHAPE 30
HEAD—Medium and shapely, with large, bright hazel eyes;
EARS—Erectly carried, medium thick, 5½ inches long, free
    from ticking; Head and Ears to match the body color.. 15
LEGS—Medium heavy boned, front feet solid reddish buff;
    hind feet red as possible 15
CONDITION—Firm in flesh and close-coated............ 10
OFFICIAL WEIGHT—4½ pounds at three months; 6
    pounds at five months; 8 pounds at eight months; 9
    pounds at ten months; 10 pounds at twelve months.

GERMAN GIANT DAPPLE (C. A. House—Rabbits and all About Them)

UTILITY RABBITS

German Giant Dapple Rabbit—Broken Color Flemish—Heavy-Weight Belgian—Flemish-Belgian Cross

WEIGHT—(Over TEN pounds)........................ 40
BODY—Large, roomy and broad fore and hindquarters.... 25
LEGS AND FEET—Strong in bone, large and straight.... 15
HEAD AND EARS—Head large, full and shapely; EYE
    bold; EARS erect and moderately thick.............. 10
CONDITION—Full short coat, firm in flesh, and free from
    cold 10

29

THE CAVY

(Courtesy The Pet Stock World Company, Baltimore)

HABITAT—DESCRIPTION

The cavy, or guinea pig, as it is commonly known, is the name applied to several South American rodent animals included in the "cavidae" family, but naturalists apply it, perhaps more properly, to the genus "cavia."

The cavy, in its wild state, is distributed over an extensive area of South America and is represented by several species: the more common being the *aperea* or *cobaya* (restless cavy) of Brazil; the Bolivian cavy, *boliviensis*, found at great elevations in the Andes Mountains; the Brazilian rock-cavy, *cavia rupestris*, characterized by its short blunt claws, and the Peruvian *cavia cutleri*, which is supposed to have been tamed by the Incas, the reigning aristocratic and priestly caste of Ancient Peru, between 1240 and 1523. This theory seems quite plausible when we consider the marvelous devlopment of the Llama which is accredited to the Incas, who regarded this animal as royal property, and almost as sacred as to India its white elephant.

The early history of the cavy is so veiled in mystery that it is questionable whether our common guinea pig descended from the specie known as *cavia porcellus* or *cavia aperea* of Brazil, the *cavia cobaya*, or the Peruvian *cavia cutleri*. Its introduction into Europe after the conquest of Peru by the Spaniards warrants the conclusion that it must have been the pet of the remarkable peoples that inhabited the fabled gold-laden country of the Andes.

The name "guinea pig" appears to be a misnomer of unknown origin, some authorities conjecturing that it is a corruption of guinea-pig; others that it was derived from the association with the English coin "guinea," for which it is said to have been sold in England during the sixteenth and seventeenth centuries; and still others that the word "guinea" merely signifies foreign.

Because of its great fecundity and the ease with which it yields to experiment the fancier has taken a keen interest in this little creature, and since the middle of the nineteenth century wonderful strides have been made in perfecting it to the standard which man thinks Nature should have adopted in its natural law of selection. From the vari-colored wild animal the patient fancier, aided by "Father Time," has produced a dozen distinct colors and combinations of the rarest hues, as well as the most freakish abnormalities, from Nature's standpoint, in its shape and length of coat. It has risen from its insignificance and humble wandering life among aquatic plants in marshy districts, and the crags in the mountain sides of South America, to the distinction of being groomed and petted by the aristocracy of the British Empire and other leaders of society throughout the civilized world.

VARIETIES

This subject is one that should stand foremost in our mind's eye. Too many of us forget the IDEAL, or the standard of perfection, which we should follow as our guide, and instead dote on some particular shade of color, shape or setting of ears, or "buffalo" shoulders, and forget the AVERAGE of all the points for which we should strive.

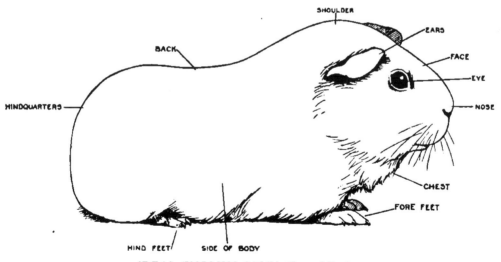

IDEAL ENGLISH CAVY (Fur and Feather)

ENGLISH

The structure of the English cavy is described by Mr. House as follows: "The English cavy must be cobby. Its head large and chubby, with a good Roman nose; the eyes should be bold, bright and prominent; the neck short, with great depth of shoulder; the back broad and massive, with well-formed hindquarters; the ears should be well set on, and droop gracefully, not enough to be styled umbrellas, but just a nice, well-turned droop. Prick ears give a rat-like appearance to the head. The coat should in all varieties be short, perfectly smooth, and very soft and silky to the touch."

In this variety we have, at present, six self or solid colors: black, red, cream, white, chocolate, and blue. The last two colors are still in their infancy, although considerable progress has been made in perfecting the same.

DUTCH MARKED CAVY (T. A. Martin, Jr.)

In the broken, or vari-colored, are the tortoise-shell (black and red), tortoise-shell and white (black, red and white), Dutch, Golden Agouti, Silver Agouti, Himalayan, and Brindle. A steady advance is also being made in producing such combinations as agouti, red and white; chocolate, red and white; and cinnamon colored. These, when eventually perfected, will create quite an interest, as they are most difficult to produce.

The BLACK cavy should be of the intense blackness of the Raven, full of lustre, with a fine, sleek coat. It is an easy matter to obtain a good outer coat, but the deep black color should extend to the skin.

The RED cavy is described by some as a "rich, bright orange," and by others as a "tomato red." The greatest care should be exercised to keep out the mahogany color.

The CREAM should be just as its name indicates. The Englishman calls it "Devonshire" cream. It should not be too dark, as many of the creams are too near an orange color, rather than cream.

The WHITE should be snowy white, with white ears and pink eyes. Being albinos, they almost invariably breed true to color, and when so bred they usually have very pretty ears. But when crossed with a dark-colored pig the ears will have a dirty appearance. This should be avoided.

The CHOCOLATE cavy should be the color of a fresh cake of chocolate; uniformly colored over entire body, including ears, feet and toenails. The color should extend down the full length of the hair, right to the skin.

The BLUE is not only the latest color produced in the self varieties, but the least perfected as well. The shades thus far presented are too slaty, and appear to be no more than faded black. When finally perfected this will be one of the most beautiful colors obtainable in cavies.

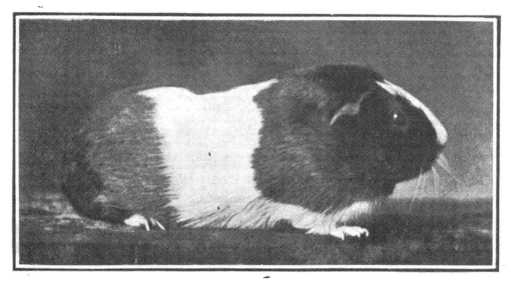

TORTOISE AND WHITE CAVY (C. A. House)

The TORTOISE-SHELL is a rarity in the United States, and in fact I learn that it is not as popular in England as the TORTOISE-SHELL AND WHITE. In the former the colors should be red and black, while in the latter white is added. There should be absolutely no brindling of colors, that is to say, intermixing, and the patches should be as numerous and uniform as possible. The tortoise-shell and white may have a one, two or three-colored face.

The DUTCH and HIMALAYAN should be marked similar to the rabbits of the same colors. The former has been bred for a longer period than the latter, hence has reached a higher state of perfection. The "Ideal Dutch Cavy" illustrated herein gives an excellent idea as to the beauty of this little creature if it could be perfectly produced. In the Himalayan all ends should be of some solid color other than white, while the rest of the body should be snowy white, free from brindling.

AGOUTI is the name applied to the variety whose color has been copied from the wild Agouti, or "Cotia," in Portuguese, native of Brazil. The wild agouti and cavy are not related, only the color of the former having attracted the inventive and imitative eye of the fancier. This variety made its first appearance in the Crystal Palace Show, London, in 1888. It is bred in two combinations, golden and grey, or silver. The former should be of a rich golden brown, while the latter a silvery grey, both evenly ticked on top, sides, chest and feet, but void of ticking on belly. In the golden agouti the belly should be rich, deep red; while in the silver agouti a pearl grey color should be attained.

STANDARD OF POINTS

ENGLISH—SELFS

COLOR—Solid and carried down to the roots of the hair, ears and feet; must match the body color............. 25
EARS—Color to match body, shapely and well carried..... 15
EYES—Large, bold 10
SHAPE—Short, cobby body, deep broad shoulders, Roman nose 20
FEET—Sound in color, to match body..................... 10
COAT—Short and silky 10
CONDITION 10

ENGLISH—TORTOISE-SHELL

PATCHES—Clear and distinct 45
EYES—Large and bold 10
COAT—Short and silky 10
SIZE, SHAPE and CONDITION—Similar to SELFS..... 20
COLOR—Black and Red, equally distributed in distinct patches, the smaller and more uniform the better...... 15

ENGLISH—TRI-COLOR

(Tortoise and White and any combination of three colors)

PATCHES—Clear and distinct 25
DISTRIBUTION—Equal; placing of patches uniform..... 10
COLOR of each patch distinct without brindling......... 20
SHAPE—Similar to Selfs 15
EYES AND EARS—Similar to Selfs 10
CONDITION AND COAT 10
SIZE 10

ENGLISH—HIMALAYANS

NOSE MARKINGS, well carried up to eye.............. 15
FEET MARKINGS, well carried up..................... 10
EAR MARKINGS, down to base....................... 10
DENSITY of markings 20
PURITY OF WHITE 15
EYES, large and bright, and of a reddish color........... 10
SHAPE, similar to Selfs............................. 10
CONDITION 10

ENGLISH—AGOUTI (GOLDEN AND SILVER)

Same requirements as Self Cavy, except ticked-color.

ENGLISH—BRINDLE (BLACK AND RED INTERMIXED)

Same requirements as Self Cavy.

IDEAL DUTCH (Fur and Feather)

ENGLISH—DUTCH

BLAZE AND CHEEKS 15
CLEAN NECK 10
SADDLE 10

35

PERUVIAN CAVY (Doubleday, Page & Co.)

PERUVIAN

The Peruvian Cavy doubtless originated in the same country as the English Cavy. It is the common belief that its outward characteristics were developed in France, and

36

later improved by the English pioneer fanciers. Length of coat, head furnishing, and texture or silkiness of coat are the principal points for which the Peruvian admirer strives. The importance of these three characteristics may be appreciated when we consider that fifty-five points out of a possible hundred are allotted to them in the standard. The Peruvian is larger than the English or the Abyssinian, while the head alone is proportionately not so large as in the other varieties. The colors produced in this variety are the same as in the other two.

STANDARD OF POINTS

SWEEP—(Length of Rear Coat)—Of as uniform length
    over all as possible.................................... 15
DENSITY OF COAT 15
TEXTURE OR SILKINESS OF COAT................. 15
SIDE SWEEP OF HAIR, as long as possible............. 15
COLOR—(Selfs, free from stray hairs; Broken, as uni-
    formly colored as possible, according to classes)....... 10
CONDITION 15
HEAD FURNISHINGS—Fringe should fall well over face,
    and shoulders should be furnished that it falls in a
    thick mane 15

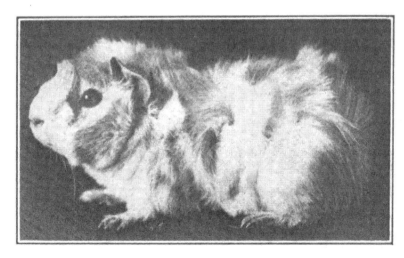

ABYSSINIAN CAVY (T. A. Martin)

ABYSSINIAN

The Abyssinian, like the Peruvian, did not derive its name by any geographical association and undoubtedly emanated from the same source as all other cavies. It has been steadily improved both in harshness of coat and the number of rosettes, which are its principal characteristics. The more numerous the rosettes the better; as many as fifteen, and rarely more, having been produced on a single cavy. Sixty points out of a hundred are devoted to rosettes, coat, and head furnishings, while only 20 points are allowed for size and shape. The attention to coat should, therefore, be paramount.

STANDARD OF POINTS

ROSETTES—Each to rise and radiate evenly all round from a clearly defined centre without any break or gap, and to be distributed regularly all over the body, the greater the number the better, providing that each is clear and distinct, without guttering or running into each other 25

COAT—Short, harsh and wiry in texture, with erect mane running right down the back from shoulders to rump, and without flatness or softness of any kind; the scruff or collar to stand erect and pass right round the shoulder without a break 20

COLOR—Clear, and bright, with plenty of lustre.......... 10

SHAPE—Short and cobby, not flat-sided; limbs well formed and closely set, without any narrowness or snippiness, with plenty of depth in shoulders and hindquarters..... 15

HEAD—Wide, and of fair length; nose very prominent, with well-developed moustache, and covered with harsh, erect coat on cheeks................................. 15

EYE—Large, full and bright 5

CONDITION—Coat close and thick, flesh firm and hard... 10

SILVER-AGOUTI ANGORA CAVY (T. A. Martin, Jr.)

PERUVIAN SILKIES (PSEUDO ANGORA)

FACE AND HEAD—Same as smooth; short Roman nose.. 20

EYES—Large, bold 10

EARS—Drooping, but not lopped............................ 10
LENGTH AND STRAIGHTNESS of hair................ 20
TEXTURE AND DENSITY of hair...................... 15
SIZE 10
CONDITION 5
COLOR 10

THE FANCY MOUSE

The fancy mouse is a thing of recent creation and credit
for its creation may be settled upon not more than a dozen
fanciers. These earnest fanciers have evolved the most
wonderful colors and markings, the most difficult results
having been obtained by the English pioneer mouse fanciers.

To Mr. W. Maxey and a few contemporaries belong the
credit for the beginning of the fancy in England. It was
he who organized the National Mouse Club of England,
which, in 1903, numbered over a hundred members, and
which now has grown to hundreds, among which may be
found the royalty as well as those in the humblest walks of
life. The same year Mr. Anton Rottmueller, of Boston,
imported America's first fancy mice. In the fall of the
same year Dr. L. H. Wood, of Groton, Connecticut, imported about thirty varieties. Prof. Thomas Hunt Morgan,
of Columbia University, then took them up and imported
many rare specimens from Europe and proceeded to cross
and recross them for experimental purposes, which, of
course, ruined their original types, but resulted in much
scientific research and knowledge.

During all of this time, and as far back as 1890, colored
mice had been sold in New York as pets for children, but
just when they were actually introduced into the pet stock
emporiums is a matter of conjecture. In 1898, Mr. S. Chichester Lloyd, of Brooklyn, commenced breeding colored
mice, since which time he has evolved several varieties,
principal amongst which are the chocolate and white, yellow
and white, tan, silver and white, etc.

Fancy mice were prominent in this country as far back
as 1904, when quite an exhibit was held at Madison Square
Garden, New York. Among the exhibitors were such per-
sonages as Miss Christine Spencer, of Staten Island; Dr.
L. H. Wood, of Groton, Connecticut; Dr. E. B. Southwick,

39

City Entomologist of New York; Prof. Charles Ellard, of Great Neck, Long Island. It was during this year also that strenuous efforts were made to push the mouse fancy, but little progress was made. In this work were interested not only those mentioned above, but such pioneer mouse fanciers as Miss Abbie E. C. Lathrop, of Granby, Massachusetts; John Block, of New York; and Mr. S. Chichester Lloyd, of Brooklyn, whose stud now numbered in the neighborhood of five thousand mice. Miss Lathrop held the office of Chairman of the Fancy Mouse Club of the American Fur Fanciers' Association until 1914, when she was succeeded by Mr. Lloyd.

GENERAL SPECIFICATIONS

MICE should be in length from seven to eight inches from tip of nose to end of tail; long head, not too finely pointed nose; large, bold and prominent eyes; large and tulip-shaped ears, free from creases and carried erect, with plenty of width between them. Body should be long and slim, and a trifle arched over loin; racy in appearance. The tail, which should be free from kinks, should come well out of the back, and be thick at the root, gradually tapering like a whip-lash to a fine end, and of about the same length as the body of the mouse. The coat should be short, perfectly smooth, glossy and sleek.

RED mice should be of a rich golden hue, both top and under color, when self or solid colors.

CHOCOLATE selfs should be the color of a cake of bitter chocolate.

BLUE selfs should be a distinct shade of slate blue, not too dark to be mistaken for blacks, but a pronouncedly different color.

BLACKS should be a very deep lustrous raven color and have no tan hairs or white feet or pied tails.

SILVERS, whether pink-eyed or black-eyed; almost white, like the white smoke of a locomotive.

WHITES must be ALL WHITE and not a yellowish tinge, whether with black or red eyes.

CREAMS, whether pink or black eyed, must be of a very light shade of yellow, and no dark or light patches anywhere on body.

PLUMS or PLUM-SILVERS must be a pronounced shade of color, about halfway between blue and chocolate. whether pink or red eyed.

AGOUTIS, which always have black eyes, must be rich brown ticked all over, with orange hairs. Rufus red in the under color.

CINNAMON, or CINNAMON-BROWNS, should be rich brown ticked, with chocolate hairs, just the color of powdered cinnamon.

GREY AGOUTIS should be about the color of a silver rabbit, ticked with brown or blue.

SABLES may be in three shades—light, medium and dark; the darker the better. From head to tail the color should be as near black as possible, shading gradually to rich gold or tan on the sides and underneath. The nose should be tan color and the hairs over the eyes tan also.

BLUE AND TANS must be a rich slaty blue on top, with tan jowls, sides and underneath.

BLACK AND TANS should be solid black on top, with a distinct dividing line on sides, jowls and feet where the tan should commence. These should also have two tiny tan specks over the eyes.

CHOCOLATE AND TANS should be of a rich dark chocolate color on back shading to tan beneath.

SILVER AND TANS should be a distinct silver color. as of a frosted silver pitcher on top, shading to deep fawn or red beneath.

TORTOISE-SHELL should be red or yellow, with distinct irregular patches of good black sprinkled over the body or face. Unless of distinct shade these mice are "sooty fawns" and merely miscolored yellows and have no value on the show bench.

SABLE AND WHITE are sables with patches of white over the body. They are known as tri-colored mice, as they are distinctly marked with black, tan and white. The more white the better the specimen.

TAN, SILVER AND WHITE are as near Dutch marked as possible, though not necessarily of this marking, having the saddle marking and hindquarters of a distinct silver shade with the under color red, while the ear and cheek

41

1 Dutch Marked   2 - Himalayan Marked   3 - Four Spotted Even Marked
4 - Even Marked   5 - Six Spotted Even Marked   6 - Seven Spotted Even - or Patched
7 - Ten Patched Broken Marked   8 - Variegated   9 - Three Patched Bald-face   10 - Banded Bald-face
11 - Holstein Marked   12 - Bald-face

IDEALS OF TWELVE VARIETIES OF MICE (S. Chichester Lloyd)

markings are deep golden red shading to silver. The rest of the body should be very white, the eyes black.

SILVER GREYS, FAWNS, BLUES and BROWNS shoud be possessed of distinct color of the shades named ticked all over with white hairs.

LILACS are nearly always pink-eyed and should suggest the shade of a lilac blossom.

PINK-EYED BLUES should be a deep blue with crimson eyes.

BROKEN MARKED—Any of the foregoing colors with black eyes irregularly patched with color on a ground of pure white are known as broken marked. In these pied tails are permissible.

Pink-eyed broken-marked mice, such as in lilac and white, silver-fawn and white, yellow and white, and cream and white, should be judged separately from black-eyed brokens and form a class by themselves.

EVEN MARKED—These have the patches of color placed evenly over a ground of pure white. (See illustrations.) They may be of any color or variety of colors, but markings must be very evenly placed.

HARLEQUIN, PATCHED or DALMATIAN MARKED mice should have a large number of spots distributed at random over the body. The more spots the better the specimen. They may be in any colors.

DUTCH MARKED mice should be as near as possible like the Dutch-marked rabbit. The higher the saddle the better, all other points being equal.

VARIEGATED mice should have tiny streaks of color, as well broken up as possible, running from head to foot and tail, all being connected by minute hair lines of color on white ground. They may be in any color.

CLASSES AND STANDARD OF POINTS

	Color	Shape, Size, Condition	Markings
Black-eyed Selfs	75	25	..
Pink-eyed Selfs	75	25	..
Dutch marked	25	25	50
Pink-eyed Brokens	75	25	..
Black-eyed Brokens, patched and variegated	25	10	65

Tri-colored or Tortoise and White..	75	10	15
Two-colored, without White.......	75	5	20
Waltzing Mice, Black and White..	25	70	5
Waltzers, Selfs	50	50	..
Waltzers, any other two colors....	50	50	..
Egyptian Spiney Mice	..	100	..
Kangaroo Mice	..	100	..
Deer Mice	25	75	..
Any other variety	50	25	25

Judges will use their discretion in deducting from each set of points any vagaries in color, shape, size and markings, the mark for condition being quite important in the case of wild mice or Waltzers, which are generally shown in poor condition.

RATS

GENERAL SPECIFICATIONS

While the rat fancy has reached large proportions in England, little progress has been made in this country. It is encouraging, however, to note that Americans are gradually awakening to the possibilities and beauties of the new varieties of rats which have recently been discovered, namely, yellows, creams, lilacs, blues and chocolates, and their broken colored brethren with ruby and black eyes.

Their tameness, sagacity and playful ways and their attachment to master or mistress makes a tame rat of beautiful color a most desirable pet, as well as the fact that a rat has absolutely none of that musky odor which is unfortunately one of the main drawbacks to the mouse fancy.

Fancy rats, crude as they were at that time, were imported as far back as 1898 by Dr. E. B. Southwick. These were nothing more than the cross between the black and the white, and the cross of the common grey house rat with the albino. Miss Lathrop also bred many rats during this time, as did also Mr. Lloyd, all of whom imported some of the new varieties of yellow rats.

An interesting feature of the rat fancy is the romantic mystery of the origin of the yellow rats. Scientists all over the world are wondering where those types came from, as the country of their nativity is unknown. They were caught on some steamer sailing either from a tropical port or from a cold climate, which is not known, as the rat-catcher did not recall the name or nationality. The original buck was a deep orange color with rich crimson eyes and killed over twenty tame does before he was finally persuaded to breed. The yellow does had black eyes and bred once and then escaped. From their progeny came all the new types. It is also understood that a Dutch scientist evolved independently an orange rat with black eyes.

The points to be considered in a rat are, mainly, color, condition of coat, tameness and freedom of disease such as snuffles, mange or eczema.

WHITES should be clear white, without yellow tinge.

AGOUTIS should be the same shade as the Agouti cavy.

BLACKS (which are usually of a deep chocolate-black) should have a deep lustre.

CHOCOLATES should be a pronounced color and not off-blacks.

BLUES are what the English term Creams. Why they are called Cream in Europe is not known, except that they are offshoots from the solid yellow rat. They are light Maltese color, with black eyes.

BLUES WITH PINK EYES—Same as above, with deep crimson eyes.

MALTESE—Light blue in shade, with either black or red eyes. Color generally white underneath.

YELLOWS, or Fawns as they are sometimes called, should be anything from a light canary to a deep golden orange, with either black or red eyes.

BROKEN MARKED or HOODED RATS—These may be any of the above colors, with or without red eyes, marked as illustrated on white ground color. The white must be distinct and the striping along back solid thin pencil line with squarecut- hood.

Rats having line along back marked with serrated edges or series of small separated spots are known as BROKEN MARKED.

CREAM AND WHITE HOODED RATS are of light chocolate color marking on white.

45

CHOCOLATE AND WHITE HOODED RATS are of cocoa color on white. Deeper colors in these varieties should be striven for.

IDEAL JAPANESE RAT (S. Chichester Lloyd)

CLASSES AND STANDARD OF POINTS

	Color	Condition	Tameness	Markings
Pink-eyed Selfs	50	25	25	..
Black-eyed Selfs	50	25	25	..
Pink-eyed Hooded	50	10	15	25
Pink-eyed Brokens	50	10	15	25
Black-eyed Hooded ...	50	10	15	25
Black-eyed Brokens ...	50	10	15	25
Any other variety of WILD OR FANCY RAT	50	5	30	15

As fanciers now have something upon which to work in the newly discovered yellows and orange, chocolate, maltese and blues, the severest penalty should be imposed upon ANY OTHER THAN TAME RATS, as no judge relishes the vicious attack of the formerly shown wild varieties, and the only necessity on the part of the breeder is daily handling of all rats.

ALL RAT CAGES USED FOR EXHIBITION PURPOSES MUST BE PLAINLY MARKED FOR THE JUDGE'S information, as to the nature or disposition of the occupant, as "TAME," "SEMI-WILD," "VICIOUS," "WILD," or other information as to the best manner of handling to judge, if necessary. THIS IS IMPORTANT.

Judges are cautioned that in judging mice or rats, particularly rats, the only safe method is to grasp them halfway up the length of the tail and swing quickly to the arm or wrist, allowing the four feet to rest thereon. Do not keep suspended in air any longer than absolutely necessary, as rats can climb their own tails. Also, if taken hold of too near the tip, the tail-skin will pull off.

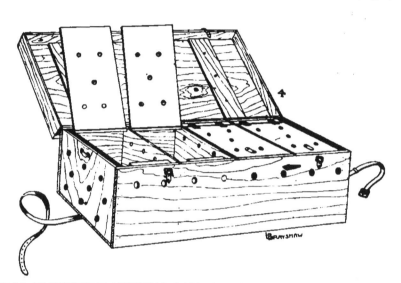

IDEAL EXHIBITION SHIPPING BOX (C. A. House—Rabbits and all About Them)

Rabbit Exhibition Box.—Ventilation is provided for by the holes bored in the ends and along the top of each side. A false end is fixed inside about one-half inch from each end, to prevent draughts.

EXHIBITING

Exhibiting is the result of the efforts of the fancier in following the advice of his older brethren; the rules laid down for the housing, breeding, and feeding of his stock; and his own practical experience. It is the zenith of his ambitions and the tell-tale of his success or failure. Temporary misfortune on the show bench should not discourage the novice, for it may be merely his inability to judge his own stock, in making his various matings, or lack of experience in any one of the several departments of the pet stock fancy, that causes him to be beaten. Success is bound to come to the observing breeder, coupled with common-sense methods. The ambitious fancier will visit the shows and acquaint himself, by kindly inquiry of the judges and well-informed veterans, wherein his shortcomings are manifest. He will return to his little family of quadrupeds and apply the knowledge thus conveyed to him, and when

47

the next season returns, to his utter amazement, the laurels find their way to this patient, persevering lover of industry.

His success should not tempt him to over-exhibit or to greedily seek to "corner" all the prizes on his several varieties, for after a few shows his stock will succumb to the strain of travel, rough handling, close and foul confinement, unsystematic feeding, and his season is closed. On the other hand, he should plan his exhibits so that sufficient time elapses between events to allow the show specimens to recuperate so that when their turn again arrives they may be able to meet the jealous pride of some fellow-animal.

The cautious fancier will provide himself with a good conditioning mixture, and feed only the most appetizing foods at these times, both before and after each show. The brush and silk or chamois skin will here demonstrate its usefulness, for the critical eye of the judge manifests his true sport by showing his preference for the well-groomed specimen. Many fanciers even supplement the brush and silk with a good rub with a whisp of hay and later with the hand, which brings the gloss to the surface. In fact, there are some who feed small quantities of flaxseed meal, which renders the hair oily and facilitates the production of the shiny coat.

In the case of white specimens, washing a few days before a show might not be amiss.

When shipping animals to distant cities for exhibition purposes, do not use any old store box that may be available. Such boxes are not only irritating to the show attendants and may subject the animals to careless treatment as a consequence, but are subject to improper handling by railroad employees. A little time and judgment may be well spent in making a case out of light wood, with a compartment for each specimen, good ventilation, and carrying handles. Each compartment should have a bountiful supply of hay before shipping, and, in addition, a carrot or two, and a piece of stale bread. Also, see that the exhibits are shipped in good time, so that all time and trouble in their rearing and preparation may not be wasted by their late arrival and consequent elimination from competition.

SHOW RULES OF THE AMERICAN FUR FANCIERS' ASSOCIATION

1. Permission may be granted to all exhibition or show committees to hold shows under these rules by application to the Governing Board, through the Secretary-Treasurer, the application to guarantee the observance of these rules.

2. Every specimen entered in competition must be the bona-fide property of the exhibitor and must be entered in the name of the owner or owners, otherwise entry fee and prize money shall be forfeited.

3. The Association shall be assured that at all A. F. F. A. shows a responsible handler is in charge, who shall supervise and be held responsible for the proper penning and care of stock and its proper return. Handling of stock shall not be permitted except by handlers, the Judge approved by the Governing Board, or the owner. Judges shall not unpack and cage any exhibition specimen.

4. Any exhibitor interfering with or interrupting the Judge during the process of judging or making himself obnoxious to Superintendent or Judge before or after judging shall forfeit entry fee and all awards and prizes on stock entered by him at the show, or if without entry and a member of the Association, shall be disciplined by the Governing Board in such manner as may be deemed proper. Disqualified exhibitors shall be reported by the Judge to the Secretary of the Association for appropriate action of the Board.

5. Any exhibitor may protest in writing for palpable dishonesty or fraudulent practice of any Judge or Judges in connection with classes in which he may be personally interested, which protest must be handed to the Secretary of the SHOW before the close of the show. The protest will be accompanied by two dollars, which shall be forfeited if protest is not sustained by the Governing Board, but will be refunded if sustained.

6. No judge shall exhibit in any class he is assigned to pass upon at any show.

7. Judging shall be by COMPARISON.

8. Exhibitors may have individual specimens scored by the Association Standard upon payment of 25 cents for

each specimen. Requests for scoring must be included on entry sheet at time of submitting entry.

9. The American Fur Fanciers' Standard of Perfection shall be the authority on all points involved in the judging of specimens under these rules. Any judge wilfully deviating therefrom shall be disqualified by the Governing Board, upon proof thereof signed by at least three exhibitors and the Secretary of the Show.

10. Any exhibitor of pet stock showing or competing under these rules who may not be a member of this Association shall submit and hereby agrees to submit to the jurisdiction of the American Fur Fanciers' Association, and shall be treated in like manner as any member. The presence of exhibits shall constitute compliance herewith and acquiescence with these rules.

11. SENIOR class is for all rabbits, cavies and mice not included in the JUNIOR class. JUNIOR class is for all RABBITS under six (6) months old, and cavies under four (4) months old WHEN EXHIBITED. BROOD class is open to does and sows with litters under ten weeks and over three weeks' old. In case of doubt as to age of specimen, the Judge shall exercise his discretion and shall have the advantage of the doubt in passing upon same.

12. All specimens shall be exhibited in their natural condition.

13. When specials are offered for the best of a variety or the best animal in a show, all first prize animals in that particular variety, or, if offered for the best animal of any variety in the show, all prize winners shall be considered, and the one scoring the highest general average, without regard to breed or variety, shall be awarded the prize.

SPECIAL AWARDS on sweepstakes shall be made on points, first prize to count 6; second, 4; third, 3; fourth, 2, and fifth, 1. Pens to count double. The total number of points won by an exhibitor to be MULTIPLIED by the number of specimens exhibited in his variety. This grand total to be the number of points counted in the competition.

14. The term BREEDER is defined by OWNERSHIP of FEMALE at the time of mating.

15. Classes shall be provided for Senior Male, Senior Female, Junior Male, and Junior Female, for the following varieties:

RABBITS

Belgian Hares	New Zealand	French Lop
Angora, White	Dutch, Black	Polish
Angora, A. O. C.	Dutch, Blue	Silver Grey
Himalayan	Dutch, Steel	Silver Fawn
Flemish Giant (Steel Grey)	Dutch, A.O.C.	Silver, A.O.C.
	English, Black or Blue	Blue Imperial
Flemish Giant, A.O.C.	English, A.O.C.	Any other variety
Black or Blue and Tan	English Lop	

Rabbit Utility Department

Best Utility Rabbit for table purposes.

CAVIES

Separate Classes Will Be Provided for English, Abyssinian and Peruvian

Self Black	Self Chocolate	Black Dutch
Self White	Golden Agouti	Red Dutch
Self Red	Silver Agouti	Any other color
Self Cream	Tortoise and White	

Angora Cavies—Any Self color, and any Broken color

MICE

Black-eyed Selfs	Tortoise and White	Waltzers, any other two colors
Pink-eyed Selfs	Two-colored, without White	
Dutch Marked		Egyptian Spiney
Pink-eyed Broken	Waltzing, Black and White	Kangaroo
Black-eyed Broken, patched or variegated	Waltzers, Self	Deer Mice
		Any other variety

RATS

Pink-eyed Selfs	Pink-eyed Broken	Any other variety of Wild or Fancy Rat not enumerated in Standard or newly discovered
Black-eyed Selfs	Black-eyed Hooded	
Pink-eyed Hooded	Black-eyed Broken	

16. The show rules of any fair, show, or other exhibition in which pet stock is entered in competition under these rules shall govern where not in conflict herewith.

INDEX

Made in the USA
Las Vegas, NV
16 January 2023